BLOCK ALPHABETS
IN
SPLIT RING TATTING

Enjoy!
Karen Bovard

KAREN BOVARD © 2015

Published by: The ShuttleSmith Publishing Company
9102 Poppleton Avenue
Omaha, Nebraska 68124   USA

www.TheShuttleSmith.com

theshuttlesmith@gmail.com
k.bovard@yahoo.com

D1737843

ISBN: 978-0-9835441-2-8

© Karen Bovard 2015 All Rights Reserved

Block Alphabets in Split Ring Tatting

Karen Bovard © 2015

A one-room country schoolhouse is how I grew up. I spent 8 and a half years in one in rural, northeast Nebraska--kindergarden through eighth grade. I felt I was well schooled in the 3 R's of Reading, wRiting, & aRithmetic. My school *(just like in the interior photo below)* had a line of block letters in the front of the classroom, my formative introduction to the alphabet. My first teacher, Mrs. Chambers, would have been proud of my use of her lessons to create a new approach to a set of alphabets in the form of what is found in this book: *Block Alphabets in Split Ring Tatting*. I have other tatting ties to my one-room schoolhouse. It was where my father and my grandfather attended school too. At one point, my grandfather *(a Nebraska farmer--as was my father)* confessed to me that he had learned to tat at good old District 40 Schoolhouse! He told me that when he was a child, the Nebraska winters were too harsh for the kids to go outside...so the teacher at one point taught them to tat! Imagine that!

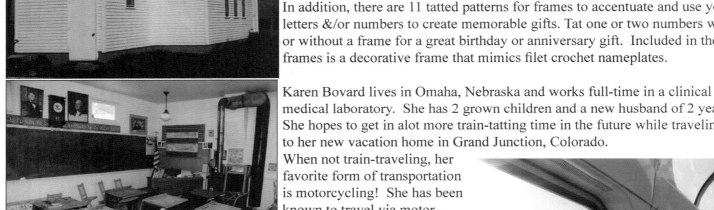

Now, a few years later, I am sharing my memories of my one-room schoolhouse upbringing and education to you in the form of this collection of two different block alphabets charted in split ring tatting technique.

There are two sizes/styles of block alphabets & numbers:
1. 7 rings high by 5 rings wide--a very simple, clean set of letters/numbers that tat up very quickly.
2. 10 rings high by 8-10 rings wide--a somewhat more elegant set of letters/numbers that feature serif attributes.

In addition, there are 11 tatted patterns for frames to accentuate and use your letters &/or numbers to create memorable gifts. Tat one or two numbers with or without a frame for a great birthday or anniversary gift. Included in these frames is a decorative frame that mimics filet crochet nameplates.

Karen Bovard lives in Omaha, Nebraska and works full-time in a clinical medical laboratory. She has 2 grown children and a new husband of 2 years. She hopes to get in alot more train-tatting time in the future while traveling to her new vacation home in Grand Junction, Colorado.

When not train-traveling, her favorite form of transportation is motorcycling! She has been known to travel via motorcycle to teach & attend tatting workshops!

Follow Karen on her blog & website at: www.TheShuttleSmith.com

Karen is available to teach a variety of tatting & other lacemaking techniques. Check out some ideas at: http://theshuttlesmithclasses.blogspot.com/ Let Karen custom design a class for your group that is guaranteed to challenge or just be fun.

Other books by Karen Bovard
Fun with Split Ring Tatting
MORE Fun with Split Ring Tatting

Due to be published in 2015
Quilt-Inspired Split Ring Tatting: Patchwork Designs
Quilt-Inspired Split Ring Tatting: Non-Patchwork Designs

Karen Bovard/The ShuttleSmith/Author
Tatting during an AmTrak train trip through Colorado

Guide/Key to *The ShuttleSmith's* Visual Patterns

The Following Standard Abbreviations are Used

R	=	Ring
SR	=	Split Ring
TOR	=	Take Off Ring/Thrown Off Ring

As in all Visual/Illustrated Patterns

- The first ring tatted that has a picot is when you will tat that picot.
- The ensuing ring tatted that is associated with that same picot will be a join

Key Point of Illustrated/Visual Patterns

Color of Portions/Arcs
- Each color represents one of two shuttle/thread sources.

Direction of the Arcs (from Dots to Arrowhead)
- Shows which way regular rings & the portions of split rings are worked.
- Gives direction to how the ring is to be tatted if Frontside/Backside Tatting Technique is used.
- Gives direction as to when the work is to be reversed.

Colored Letters
- Dictate which portion of a split ring is to be tatted first ('A') with regular, transferred double stitches & then the ('B') portion with untransferred, reverse-stitch double stitches.
- If a split ring does not have join or a TOR associated with it, the portions of the split ring can be tatted in any order *(colored letters will not be indicated)*.

Numbered Rings
- All the rings (regular, take off, or split ring) are numbered sequentially. The path the pattern is to be worked is to start at 'R1' & work in ascending order.

Regular Rings in Visual Patterns--Including Take Off Rings

-- The <u>dot</u> designates the starting point of the ring ●
-- The <u>arrowhead</u> designates the ending point of the ring. ◣   *(A regular ring starts & ends at the same point.)*
-- '**R**' is used to designate a (regular) ring.
-- The larger '#'/'number' (after the 'R') designates the order in which the rings are tatted & thus how the pattern is worked.
-- The '#' on the inside of the arc is the number of double stitches in the ring or in that particular portion of the ring and/or between picots & joins.

A regular-tatted ring in Visual Pattern style is distinquised by the fact that:
- There is only 1 arc.
- There is only 1 color used for the arc, starting dot, & ending arrowhead.
- The starting point & the ending point are at the same place on the ring.

Split Rings in Visual Patterns

-- 2 <u>dots</u> of different colors designate the starting points of the 2 different thread sources of the split ring. ●●
-- 2 <u>arrowheads</u> of different colors designate the ending points of the 2 thread sources of the split ring.
   (A split ring starts & ends at different points.) ▶◀
-- The <u>arcs</u> represent the two thread sources that create split rings.
   (When you see a ring diagram with 2 colors used, you know that it is a split ring.)
-- The abbreviations '**SR**' are used: the '**S**' meaning 'Split' & the '**R**' meaning 'Ring'.
-- The larger '#'/'number' (after the 'R') designates the order in which the rings are tatted and thus how the pattern is worked.
-- The '#' on the inside of the arcs is the number of double stitches in the ring or in that particular portion of the ring and/or between picots & joins.

When all the illustrations are put into one diagram, the complete path of the where the split ring is started, where it ends, the direction the portions of the split rings are made, and stitch counts of the portions of the split ring designate the attributes of the split ring.

Numbered Rings--Path of the Pattern

-- How the pattern is worked (or the 'path') is designated in Visual Patterns by the number inside the rings next to either **R**, **SR**, or **TOR**.
-- Start at R1 and then progress numerically (1 then 2, then 3, then 4.....) through the pattern.
-- There may be different ways or paths to take to tat the pattern other than the one illustrated. However, the patterns have been carefully designed & charted to lessen the complexity of the pattern & to allow for the following conditions:
- The pattern can be worked continuously, from start to end, in one round, or as few founds as possible.
- Regular joins (not Split Ring Joining Technique) can be used.
  --Regular joins can only be made on the *first* portion of a split ring *(the regular, transferred double stitches)*.
- Take off rings (TOR's) can be created without the need for an additional thread source.
  --TOR's are created on the *second* portion of the split ring *(the untransferred, reverse-stitch double stitches)*.
  --TOR's *(which are regular rings)* allow regular joins to be used.
- Regular rings are used as often as possible.

Colored Letters in Visual Patterns

-- Some of the split rings in the visual patterns will have colored letter designations (*inside the ring, and next to the stitch count*) and some will not.

-- If a split ring does not have a join or take off ring associated with it, the portions of the split ring can be tatted in any order.

 This split ring pattern can be tatted in one of two ways--either choice appropriate:

1. The 12-stitch (green) portion can be tatted first with regular, transferred stitches and then the 4-stitch (red) portion is tatted with reverse, untransferred double stitches.   **OR**
2. Tat the 4-stitch (red) portion first with regular, transferred stitches and then the 12-stitch (green) portion is tatted with reverse, untransferred stitches.

However, the order in which the split ring portions are tatted in some split rings is important for two reasons:

1. To create joins utilizing traditonal tatting joining technique--NOT Split Ring Joining Technique (*which is more cumbersome to master and does not create as 'neat' a join*).
    -- Done from the ***first portion*** (the regular, transferred double stitches)
2. To be able to create Take-Off Rings (TOR's) without the need to use a third thread source.
    -- Done from the ***second portion*** (the reverse, untransferred double stitches)

 This split ring pattern dictates that the 12-stitch (green) be tatted first with regular, transferred stitches and then the 4-stitch (red) portion is tatted with reverse, untransferred double stitches.

Just like in the alphabet, 'A' comes before 'B' and thus the 'A' portion is done first.

Direction of the Line Arcs (from dot to arrowheads)

-- Shows the direction that the ring is worked.

-- Shows which way regular rings and the portions of split rings are worked.

-- Gives clues/direction to how the ring is to be tatted if Frontside/Backside Tatting technique is used.

    -- If the arc of a regular ring is '*clockwise*' then the ring is tatted as a '*frontside*' ring.

    -- If the arc of a regular ring is '*counter-clockwise*' then the ring is tatted as a '*backside*' ring.

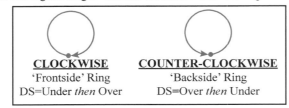

In split rings, both clockwise and counter-clockwise arcs/portions are part of each split ring.

The direction of the first portion of the split ring made dictates whether the split ring is tatted as either a 'frontside' or a 'backside' ring.

    -If Portion A is '*clockwise*' then the split ring is tatted as a '*frontside*' ring

    -If Portion A is '*counter-clockwise*' then the the split ring is tatted as a '*backside*' ring

CLOCKWISE First
'Frontside' Ring
With the 'Red' shuttle make 12 regular, transferred double stitches: *Under-Stitch-first; followed by Over Stitch*

With the 'Green' shuttle make 4 reverse, untransferred double stitches: *Over Stitch-first; followed by Under Stitch*

COUNTER-CLOCKWISE First
'Backside' Ring
With the 'Red' shuttle make 12 regular, transferred double stitches: *Over-Stitch-first; followed by Under Stitch*

With the 'Green' shuttle make 4 reverse, untransferred double stitches: *Under Stitch-first; followed by Over Stitch*

-- Gives clues/direction as to when the work is to be reversed. (*Illustrated patterns do NOT give written directions as to when to Reverse Work or Turn.*)

 If you tat one ring as a 'frontside' element (*the first portion of the split ring &/or the regular ring is a clockwise arc--**SR1***) and then the second ring is a 'backside' element (*the first portion of the split ring &/or the regular ring is a counter-clockwise arc--**SR2***) you will need to Reverse Work between these two rings.

What is a Take Off/Thrown Off Ring (TOR)?

A Take Off/Thrown Off Ring is a 'regular' ring that is created/tatted in the middle of another element. In the case of the patterns in this book, it is made in steps while tatting a Split Ring. In traditional tatting (rings/chains/no split rings) a Take Off Ring would have been referred to as a 'second-shuttle element' because is was tatted in the middle of a chain element. Take Off Rings allow rings to be tatted that otherwise would have been 'orphaned'. The patterns in this book were charted so that if you tat the split ring portions in the order they are directed you can tat TOR's using only 2 thread sources. Take Off Rings are tatted as a 'unit' with the split ring it is associated with.

All the Rings in this Book are Designed to be Round-Shaped

-Close the ring by pulling the working shuttle/thread downward, away from the base of the ring.
- Use your fingers to push the ring into a round-shape.

All Rings are Tatted with No-Space of Thread Between Rings

-The visual effect of the pieces in this book is that each ring is closely adjacent to its neighboring ring(s).
-All rings are started as close to one another as possible. NO 'gaposis'!!!

Picot Size--Use of Joining Picots

-The pieces were designed with the idea that all the rings lie in close relationship with one another.
-The picots used in this book are all examples of Joining Picots.
-Joining picots are minute picots that barely allow for insertion of a tiny crochet hook. They are used only for joining, not as ornamental picots. A Joining Picot is barely recognizable as a picot loop.
-A space of thread between the two double stitches that is creating the properly-sized Joining Picot is equal to one double stitch width.
-In the process of facilitating very tight joins between rings, very small joining picots are created. A small-gauge crochet hook is necessary to facilitate these joins.
-Proper Joining Picot size is actually so small that at times it maybe dificult to get even a tiny crochet hook into the picot loop to use it.
At these times, a dental-pick tool or a blunt-tipped sewing needle (such as a Tapestry needle--ca. Size 20, 22, or 24--*larger # equals smaller needle*) is handy to use to pull the picots out to a sufficient size to be able to easily insert a hook into to use as a join.
-If you forgot to create a picot, all hope is not lost! Just insert your crochet hook or pick/needle between the stitches where the picot 'should be'. Pull out this horizontal space of thread and use it as a picot. Picots formed this way will be an appropriate size for joining the patterns tatted in this book.

Step by Step Instructions as to How to Read Visual Patterns

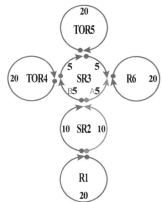

Ring 1 is a regularly-tatted ring. Only one shuttle/thread source is needed. Tat 20 regular, transferred double stitcheds and then close the ring.

The next ring in Split Ring 2 (SR2). It is an example of an 'even' split ring. To tat this ring, you will need a second shuttle/thread source. Since no colored letters are used in this illustration, either portion (the green or the red shuttle/thread source) can be tatted first/second. One way to create this split ring is to use the red shuttle/thread source to tat 10 regular, transferred double stitches. Then use the green shuttle/thread source to tat 10 reverse, untransferred double stitches. Close the ring by pulling the red shuttle/thread source.

Ring #3 is an uneven split ring (SR3) with two take-off rings associated with it (TOR4 & TOR5). These 3 rings (SR3, TOR4, & TOR5) are tatted as a unit in 6 steps:

> Step 1: With the green shuttle/thread source tat 5 regular, transferred double stitches. You know to use this shuttle/thread source because of the colored letter 'A' associated with this portion of the split ring.
> Step 2: With the red shuttle/thread source tat 5 reverse, untransferred double stitches.
> Step 3: Take Split Ring 3 off your hand. Reverse work. With the red shuttle/thread tat Take Off Ring 4 as a regular ring of 20 transferrred double stitches. Close Take Off Ring 4. Reverse work.
> Step 4: Put Split Ring 3 back onto your hand. With the red shuttle thread source tat 5 more reverse, unstransferred double stitches.
> Step 5: Take Split Ring 3 off your hand. Reverse work. With the red shuttle/thread tat Take Off Ring 5 as a regular ring of 20 transferrred double stitches. Close Take Off Ring 5. Reverse work.
> Step 6: Put Split Ring 3 back onto your hand. With the red shuttle thread source tat 5 more reverse, untransferred double stitches. Close Split Ring 3 by pulling the green shuttle/thread source.

Ring #6 is a regular tatted ring. Only one shuttle/thread source is needed. Either thread source can be used. To follow the illustration, use the red shuttle/thread source to tat 20 regular, transferred double stitches, then close the ring.

Notes on direction of the arcs of the rings & their various portions and relationship to Frontside/Back Tatting Technique & Reverse Work:
> -- *R1: the red arc is clockwise--this is a 'frontside' ring.*
> -- *SR2: depend upon which shuttle/thread source is used first. If the red shuttle/thread source is used for the first step/portion of the split ring then the arc is clockwise, thus it is a 'frontside' ring. Both portions are tatted the same way--as 'frontside' stitches. However, if the green shuttle/thread source is used first, the arc of this portion is counter-clockwise, thus the entire split ring would be tatted as a 'back side' ring.*
> -- *SR3 directs you to tat the green shuttle/thread source first. Since this arc is counter-clockwise the entire split ring would be tatted as a 'backside' ring.*
> -- *TOR4, TOR5, & R6 are all clockwise & thus are 'frontside' rings using the red shuttle/thread source.*
> -- *Because SR3 is a 'backside' ring and then TOR 4/5 are 'frontside' rings, you will need to Reverse Work when going from SR3 to TOR4 (Same for SR3 to TOR5). Another Reverse Work is needed when going from SR3 (a 'backside' ring) to R6 (a 'frontside' ring).*

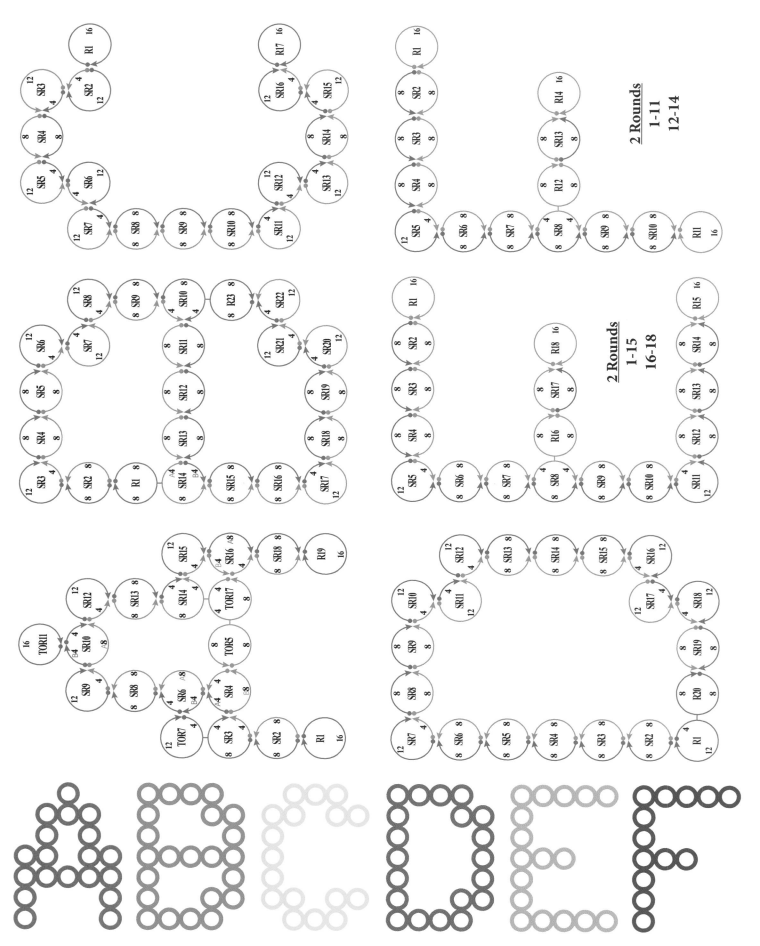

2 Rounds
1-11
12-14

2 Rounds
1-15
16-18

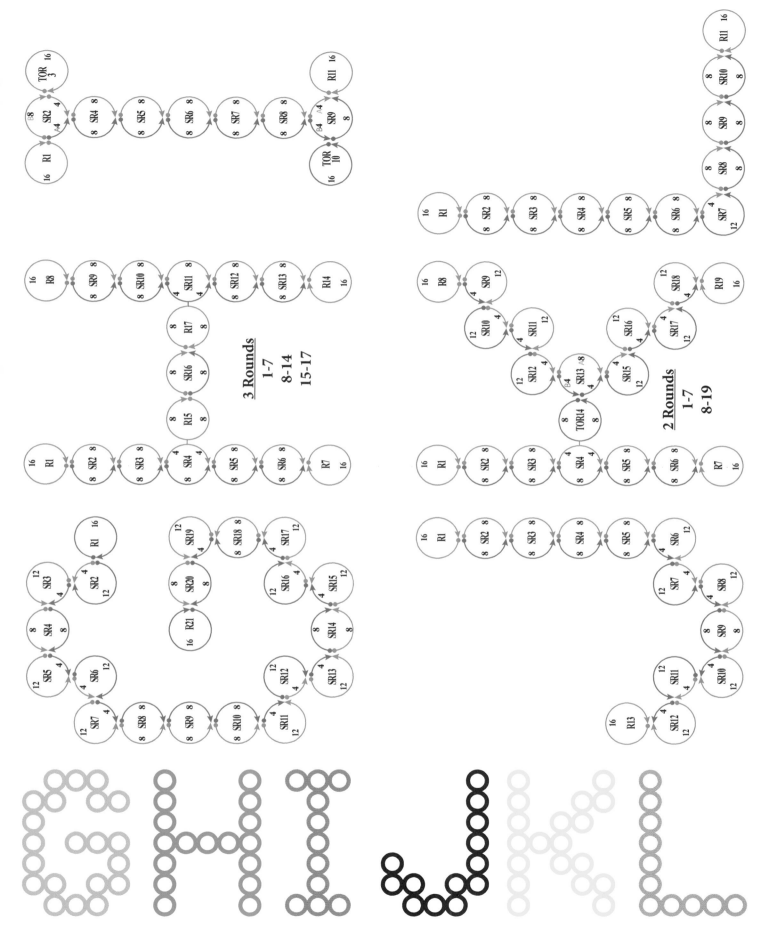

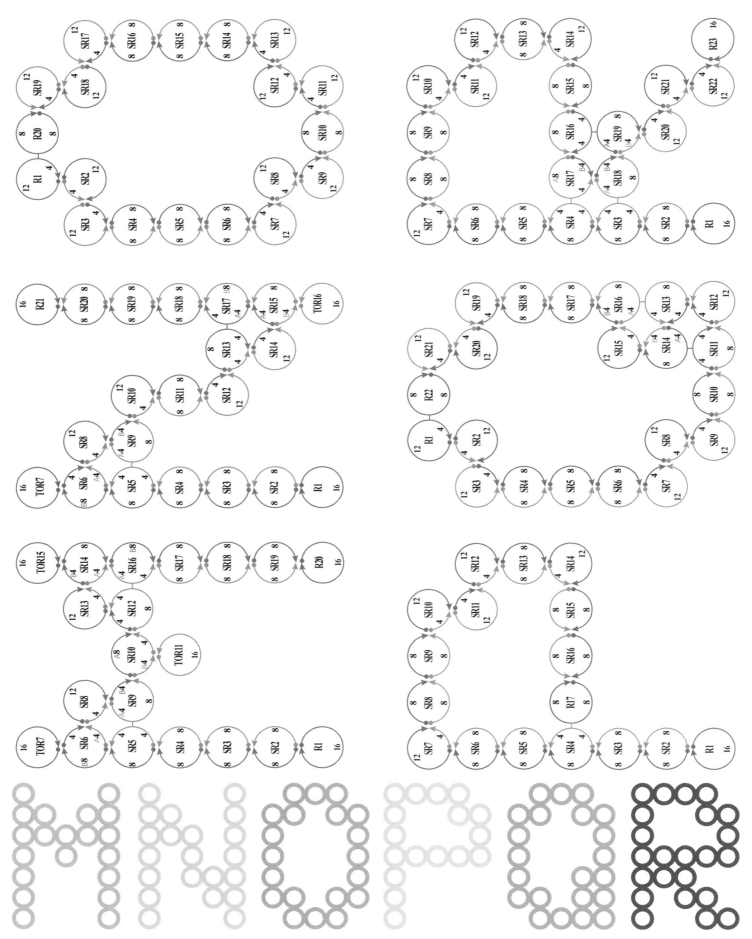

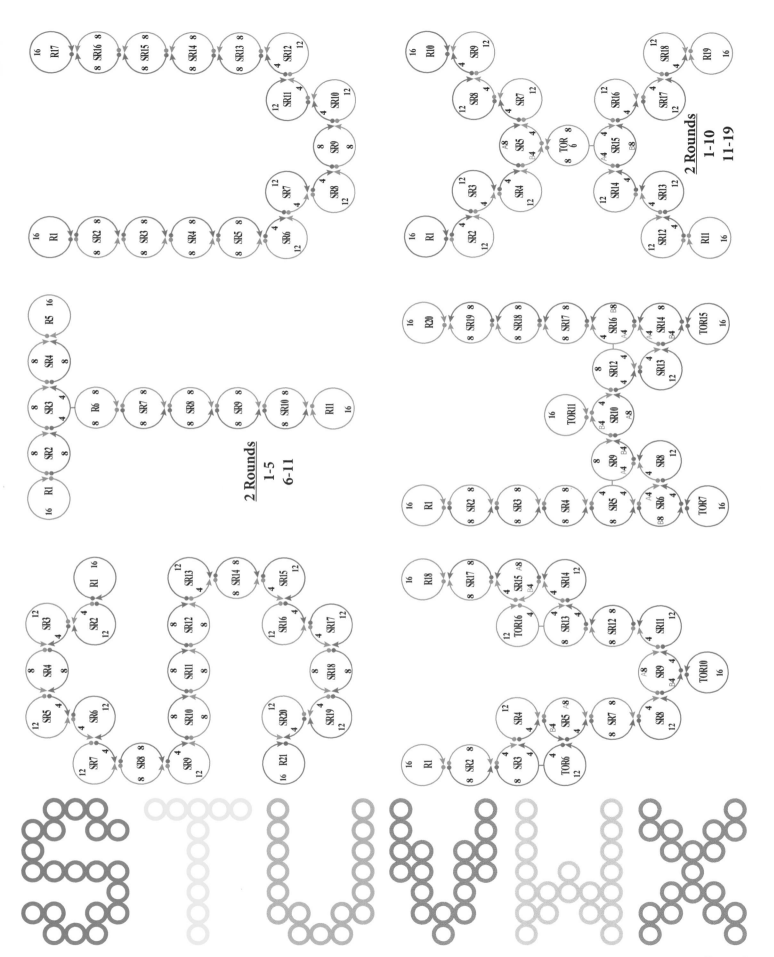

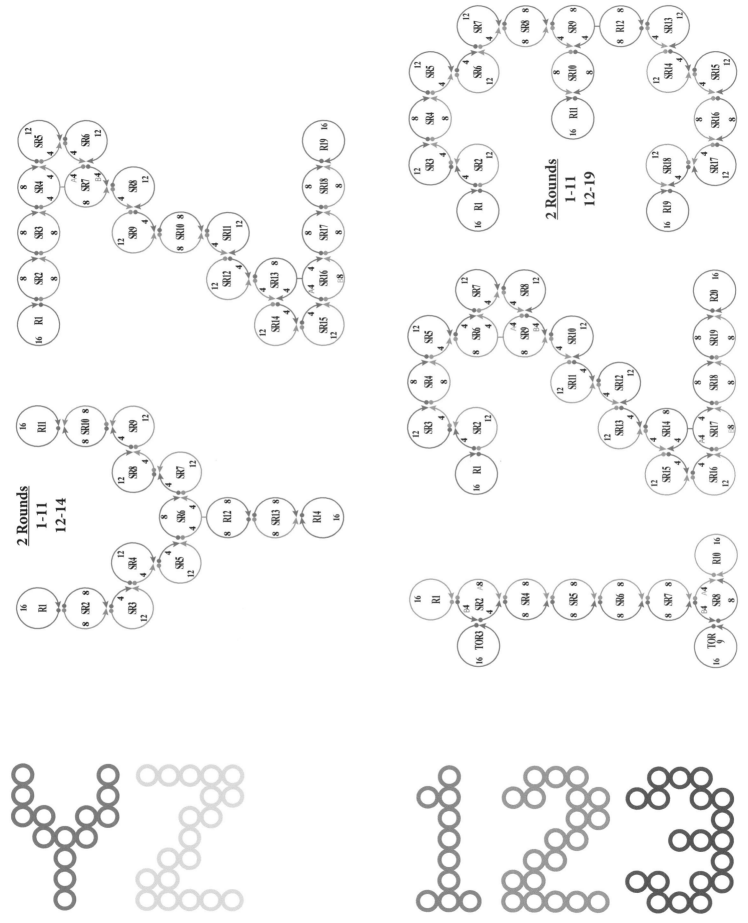

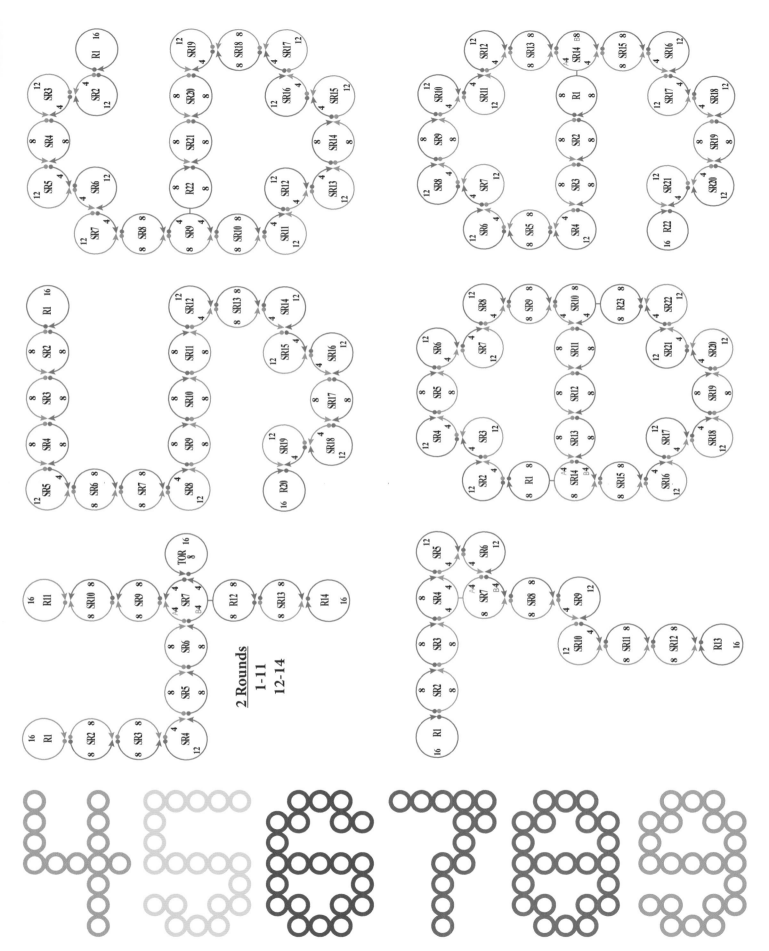

Frames for the 5x7 Letters & Numbers

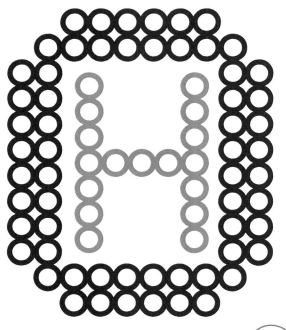

Frames A through H are created for use around the previous block alphabet letters and numbers

All letters are 7 rings high, & all letters (with the exception of 'I' & '1') are 5 rings wide.

Frame A

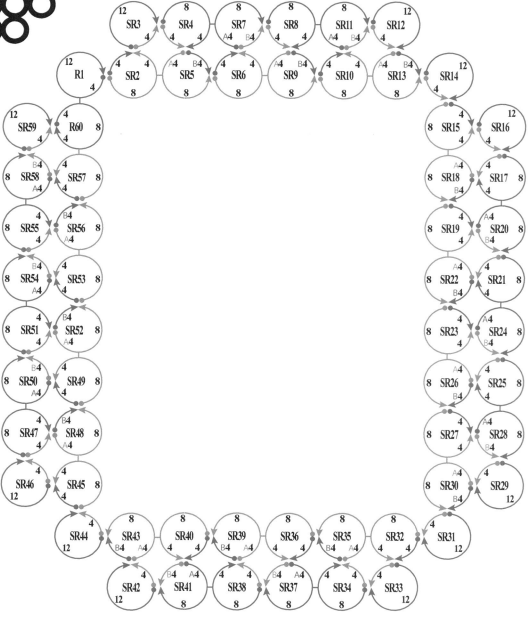

Frame B

SR3 12 4 | SR4 8 4 4 | SR7 8 A4 B4 | SR8 12 4

R1 12 4 | SR2 4 4 8 | SR5 A4 B4 8 | SR6 4 4 8 | SR9 A4 B4 8 | SR10 12 4

SR59 12 4 | R60 4 12

SR11 12 4 | SR12 12 4

SR57 12 4 | SR58 4 12

SR13 12 4 | SR14 12 4

SR55 12 4 | SR56 B4 8 A4 | SR15 8 4 4 | SR16 12 4

SR54 B4 8 A4 | SR53 4 4 8 | SR18 A4 8 B4 | SR17 8 4

SR51 8 4 4 | SR52 B4 8 A4 | SR19 8 4 | SR20 A4 8 B4

SR50 B4 8 A4 | SR49 8 | SR22 A4 8 B4 | SR21 4 8

SR47 8 4 4 | SR48 B4 8 A4 | SR23 8 4 | SR24 A4 8 B4

SR46 4 12 | SR45 4 8 4 | SR26 A4 8 B4 | SR25 4 12

SR44 4 12 | SR43 12 4 | SR28 12 4 | SR27 4 12

SR42 12 4 | SR41 12 4 | SR30 12 4 | SR29 4 12

SR40 4 12 | SR39 8 B4 A4 | SR36 8 4 | SR35 8 B4 A4 | SR32 8 4 4 | SR31 4 12

SR38 4 12 | SR37 B4 A4 8 | SR34 4 8 | SR33 4 12

Page 12

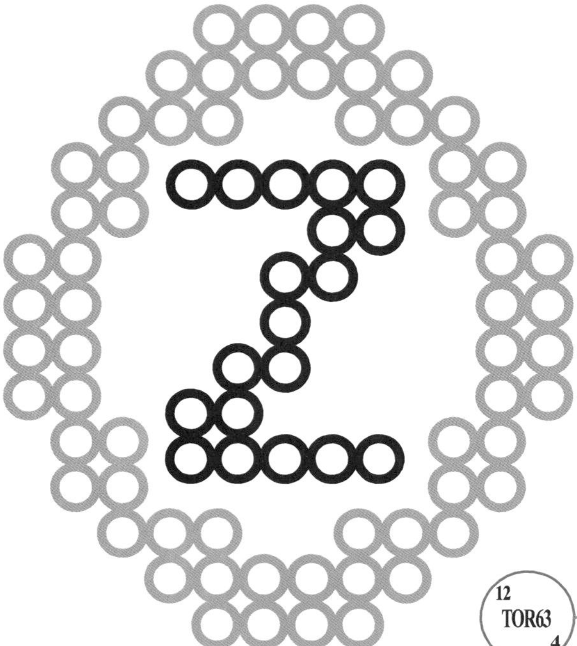

Frame C

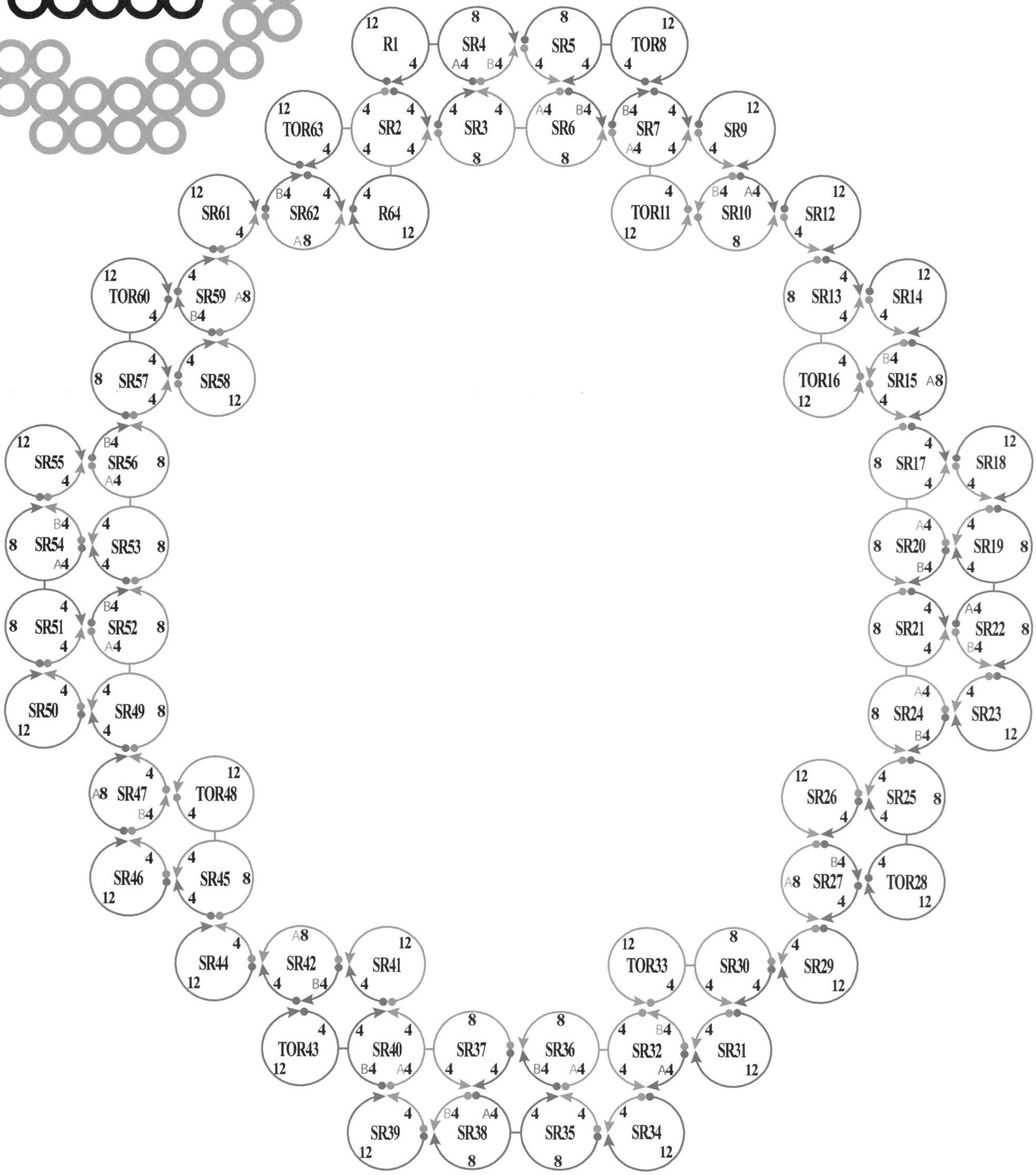

R1 12 4
SR4 8 A4 B4
SR5 8 4 4
TOR8 12 4

TOR63 12 4
SR2 4 4 4 4
SR3 4 4 8
SR6 A4 B4 8
SR7 B4 4 A4
SR9 12 4

SR61 12 4
SR62 B4 A8
R64 4 12

TOR11 12
SR10 B4 A4 8
SR12 12 4

TOR60 12 4
SR59 4 A8 B4
SR58 4 12

SR13 8 4
SR14 12 4

SR57 8 4 4
TOR16 12 4
SR15 B4 A8 4

SR55 12 4
SR56 B4 A4 8
SR53 4 4 8

SR17 8 4
SR18 12 4

SR54 B4 8 A4
SR19 4 8 4

SR51 8 4 4
SR52 B4 A4 8
SR20 A4 8 B4

SR50 4 12
SR49 4 8 4

SR21 8 4 4
SR22 A4 8 B4

SR47 A8 4 B4
TOR48 12 4

SR24 8 A4 B4
SR23 12

SR46 4 12
SR45 4 8 4

SR26 12 4
SR25 4 4 8

SR44 4 12
SR42 A8 4 B4
SR41 12 4

SR27 B4 A8 4
TOR28 12

TOR33 12 4
SR30 8 4
SR29 4 12

TOR43 4 12
SR40 4 B4 A4
SR37 8 4
SR36 8 4 B4 A4
SR32 4 B4 A4
SR31 4 12

SR39 4 12
SR38 B4 A4 8
SR35 4 8
SR34 4 12

Page 13

Frame D

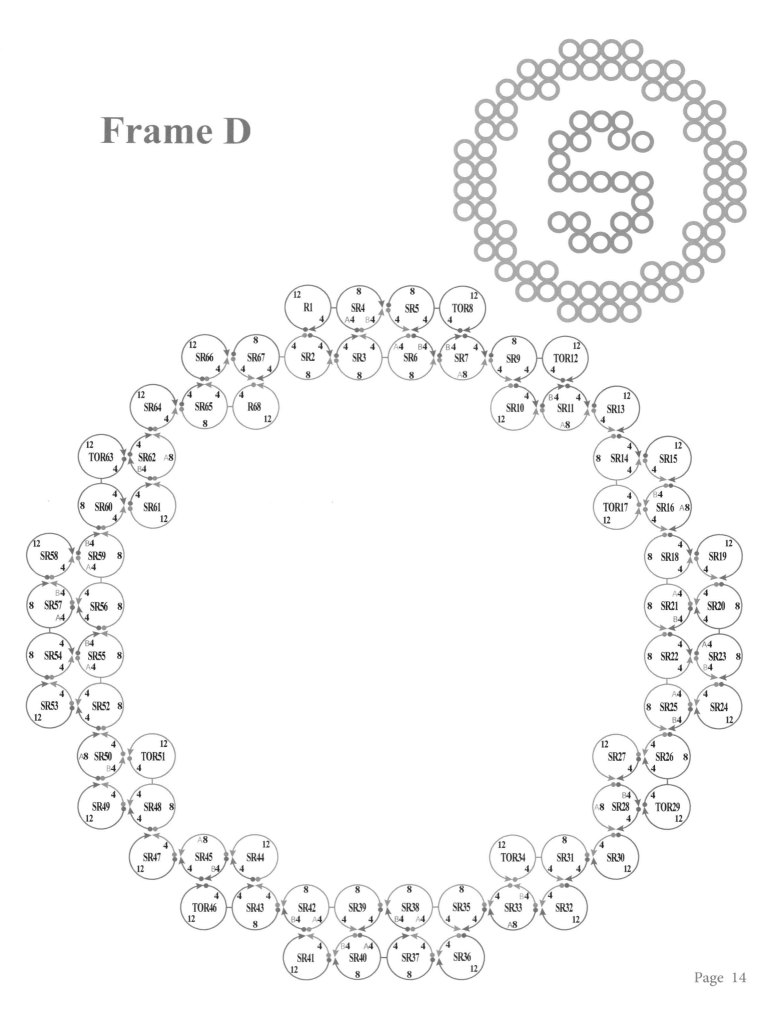

Frame E

Frame F

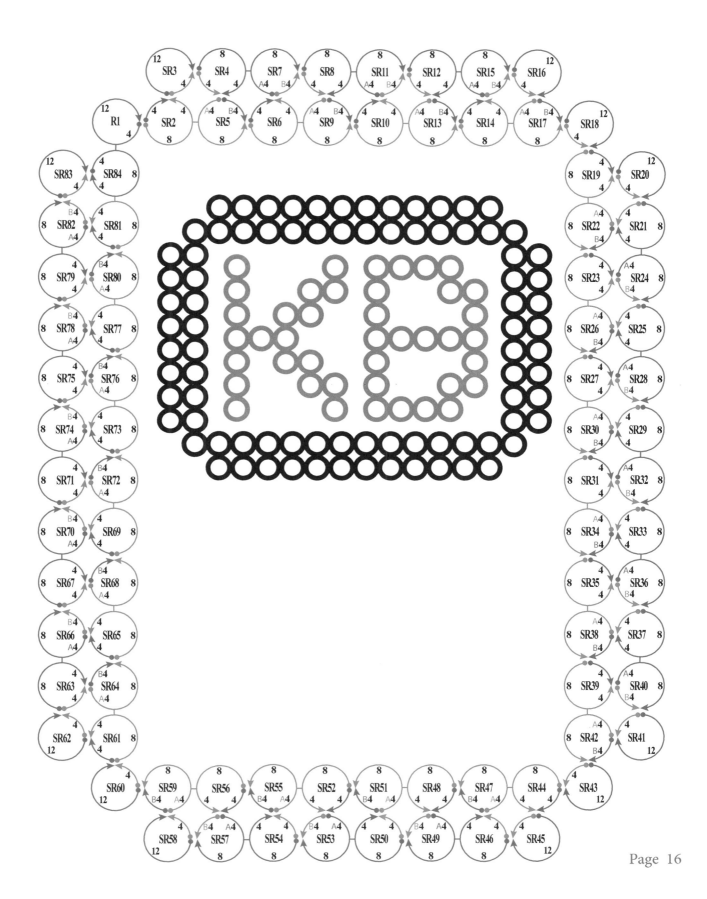

Frame G

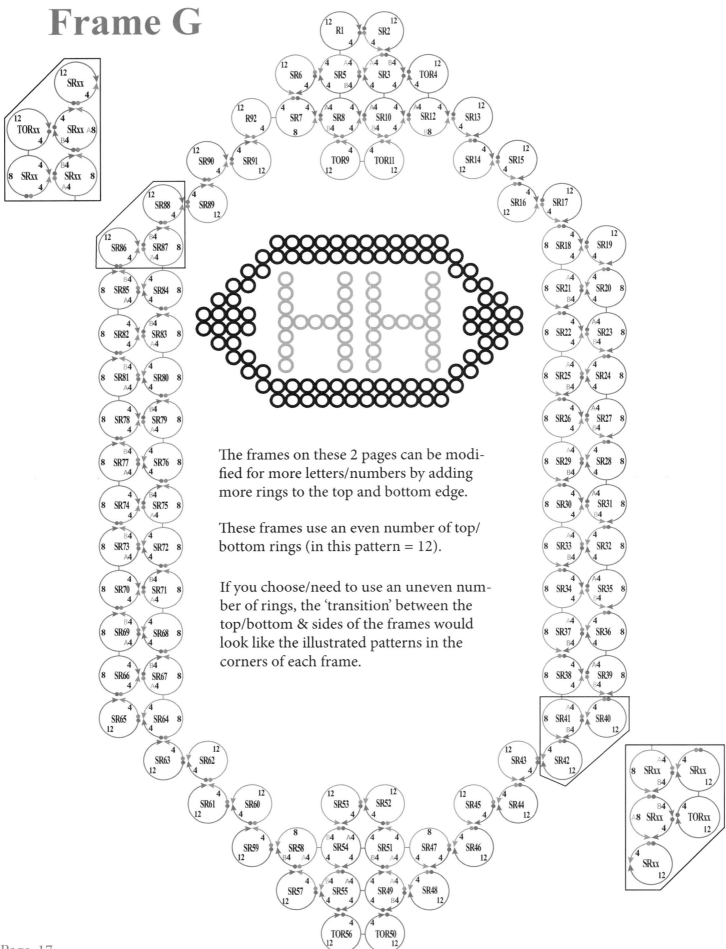

The frames on these 2 pages can be modified for more letters/numbers by adding more rings to the top and bottom edge.

These frames use an even number of top/bottom rings (in this pattern = 12).

If you choose/need to use an uneven number of rings, the 'transition' between the top/bottom & sides of the frames would look like the illustrated patterns in the corners of each frame.

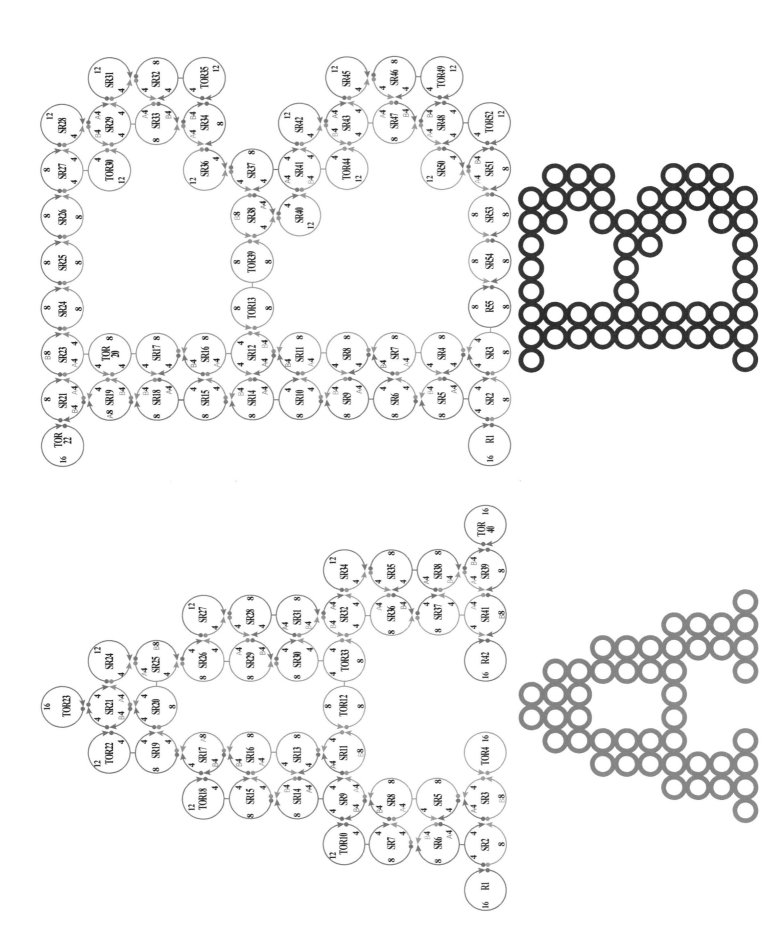

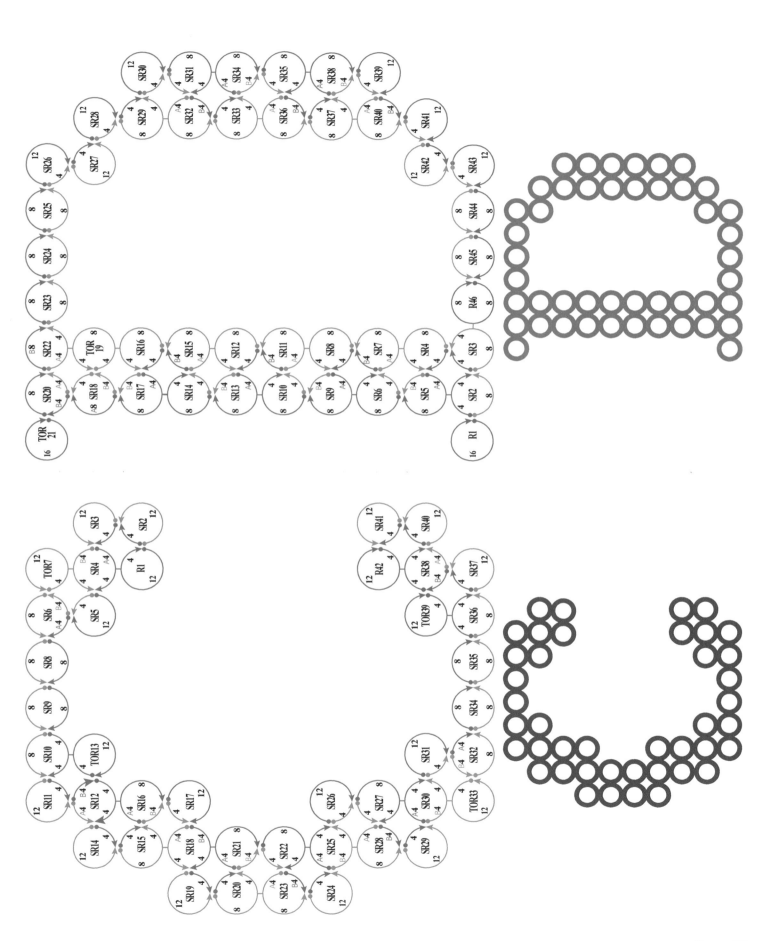

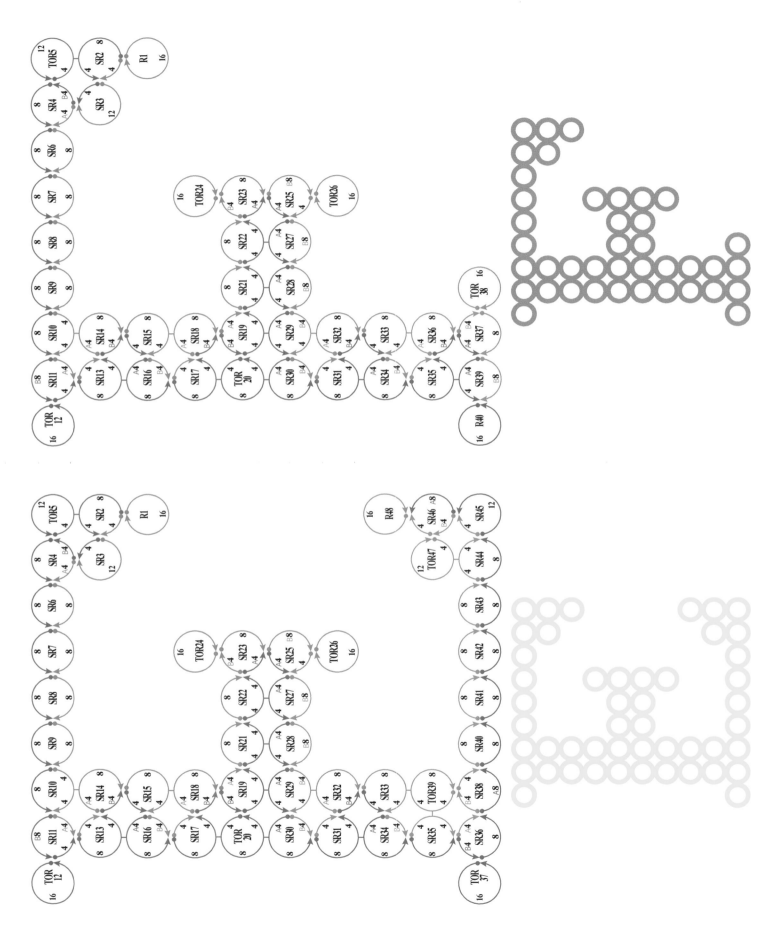

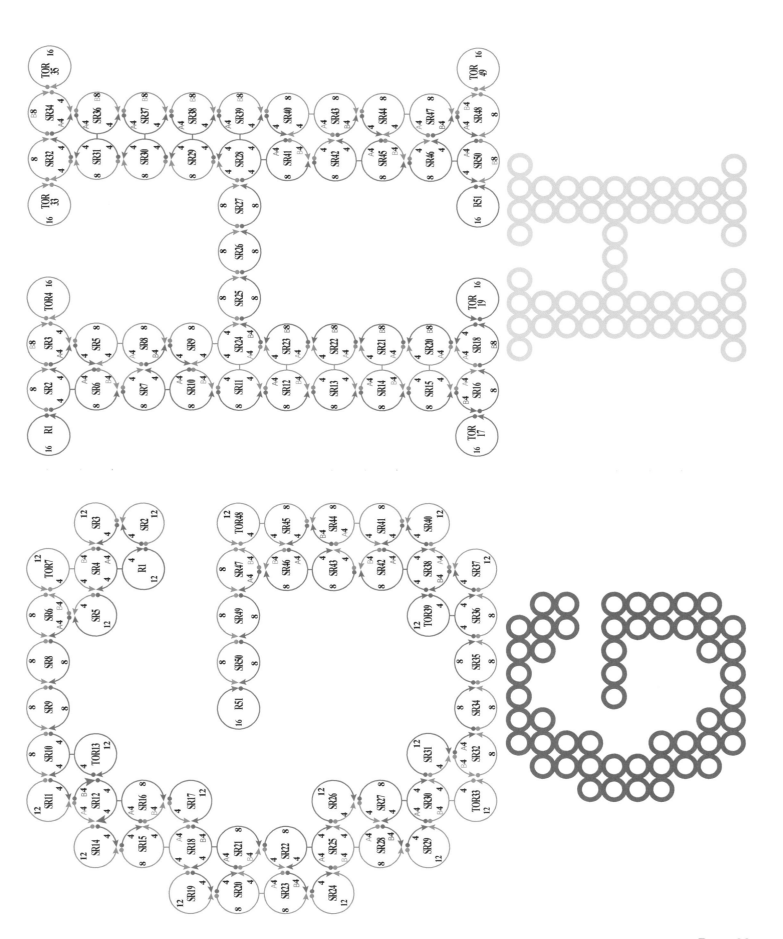

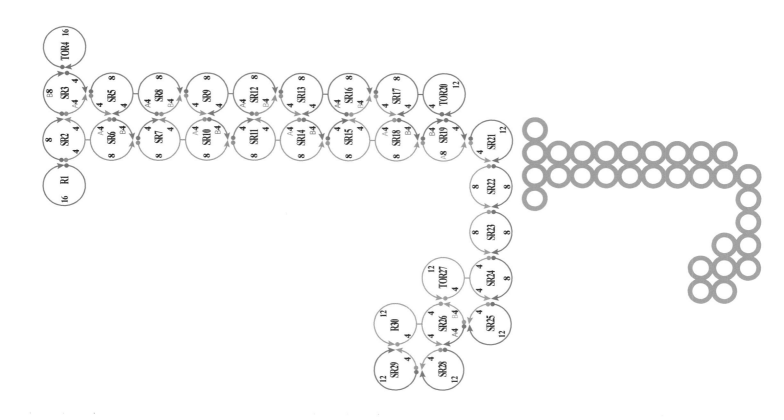

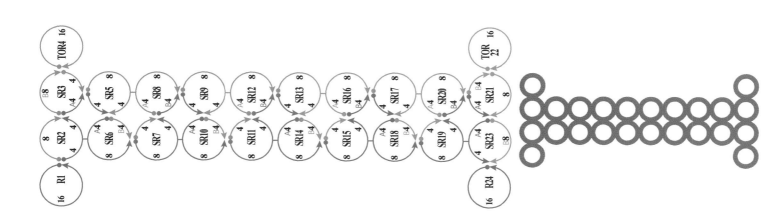

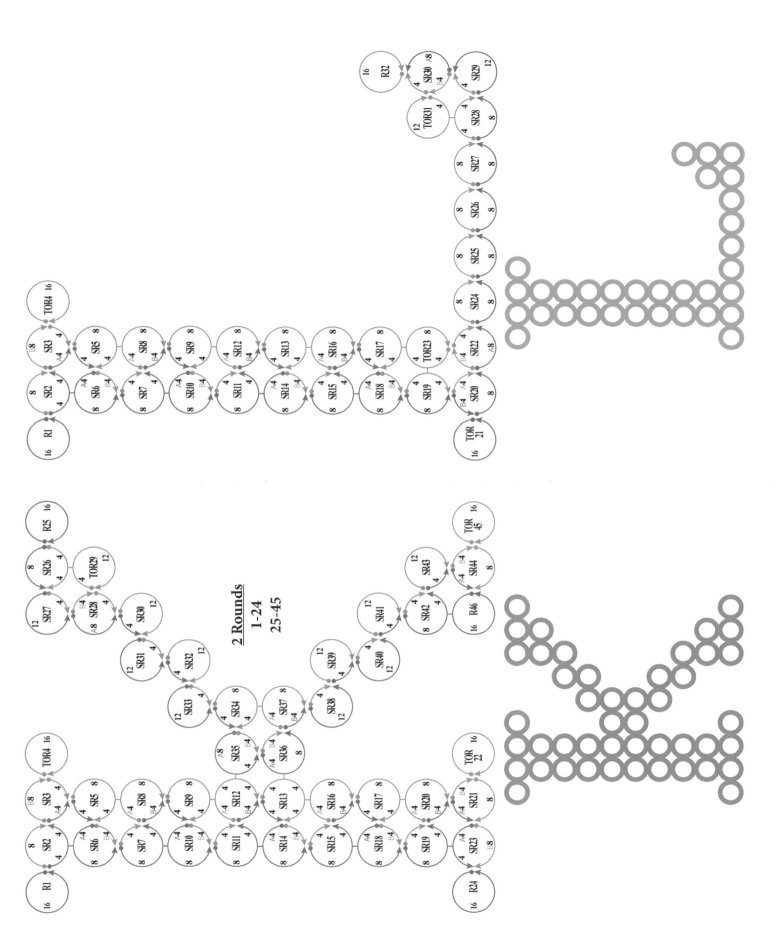

2 Rounds
1-24
25-45

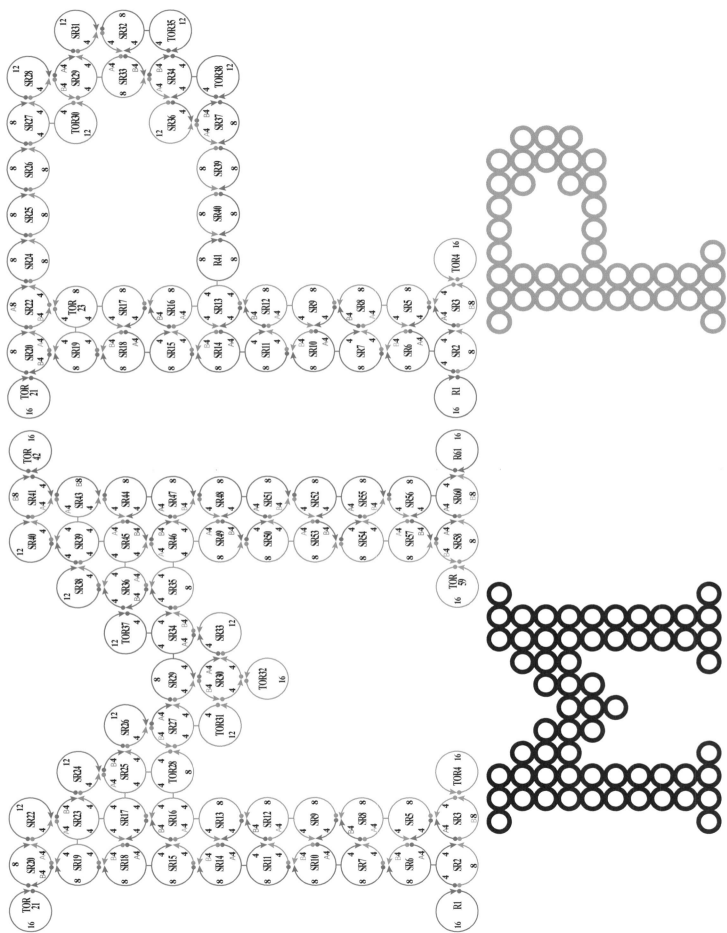

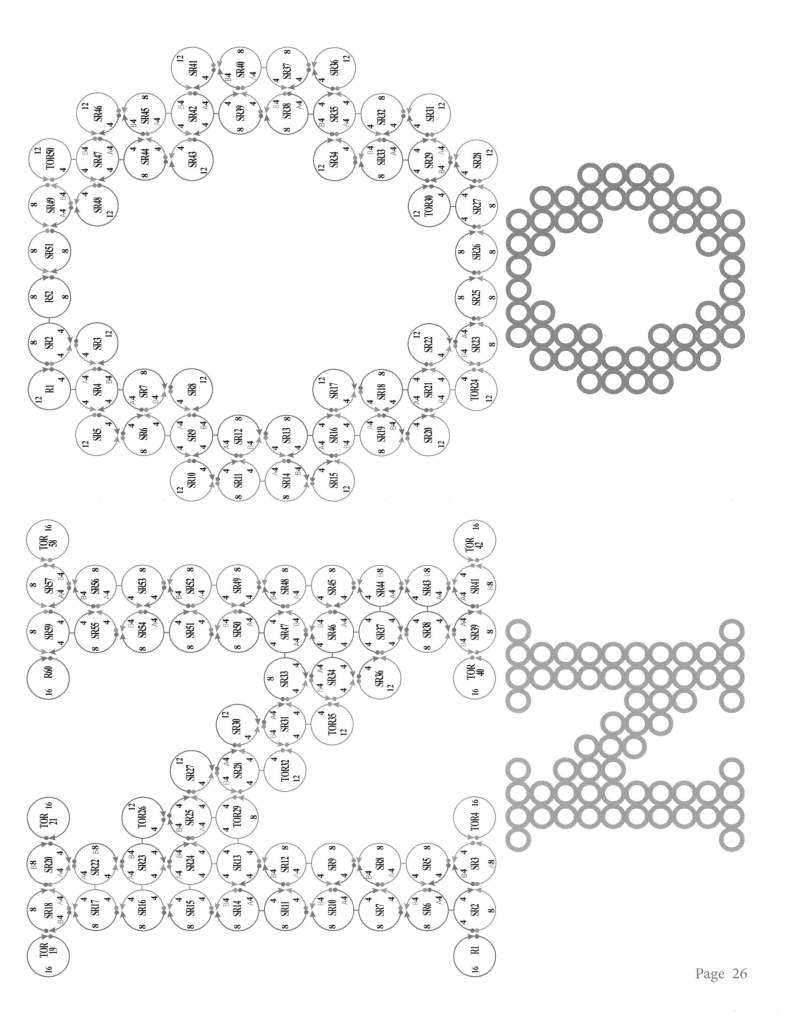

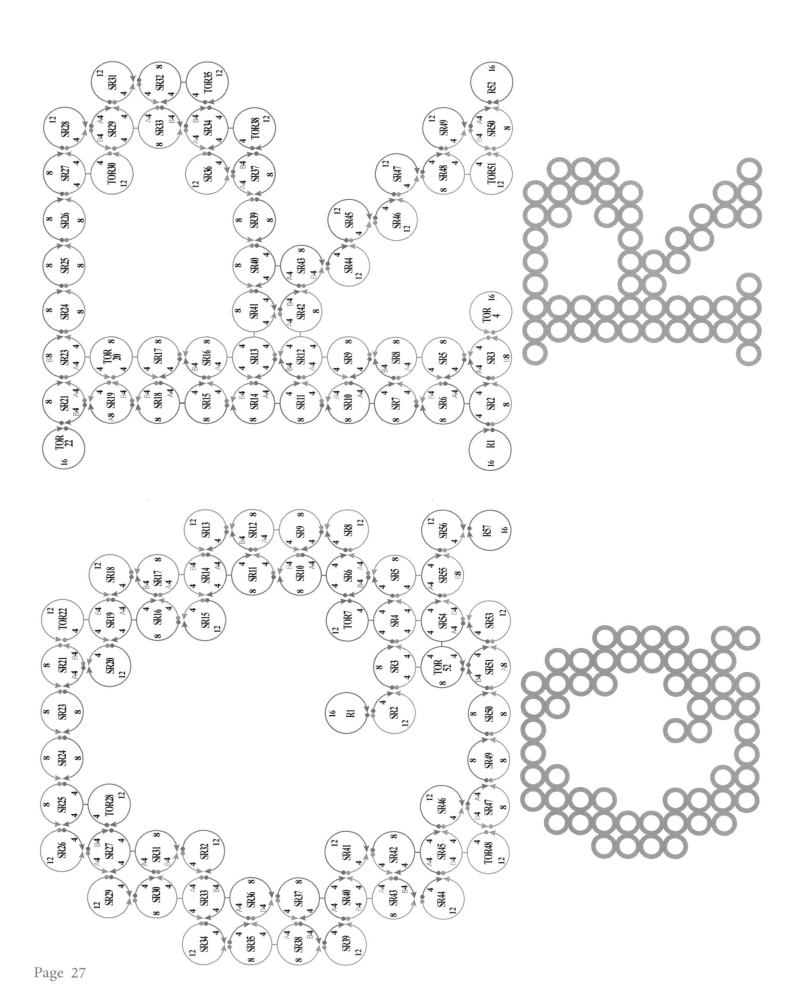

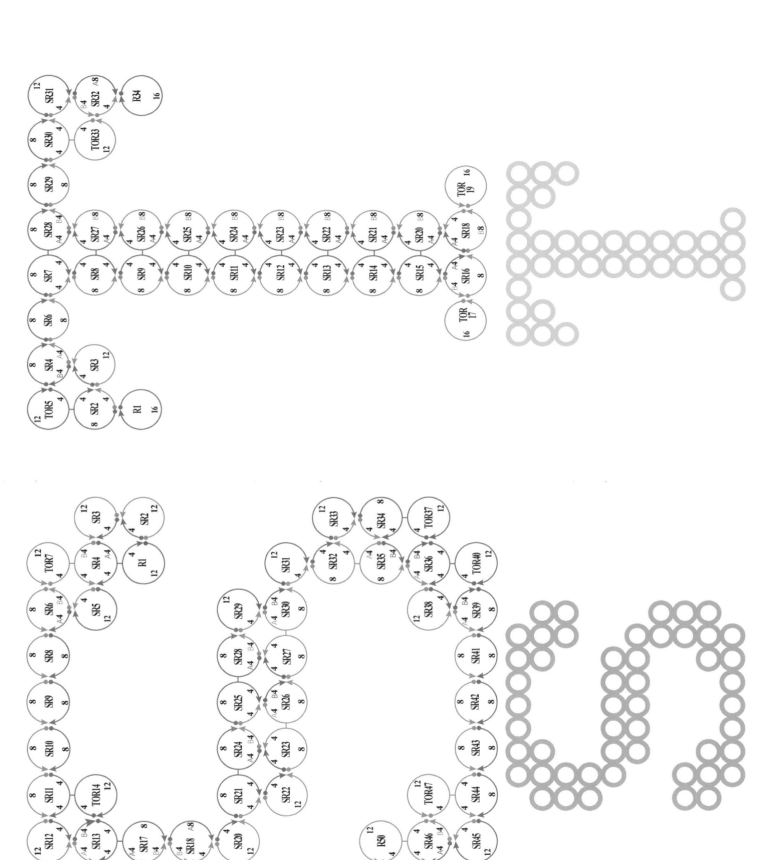

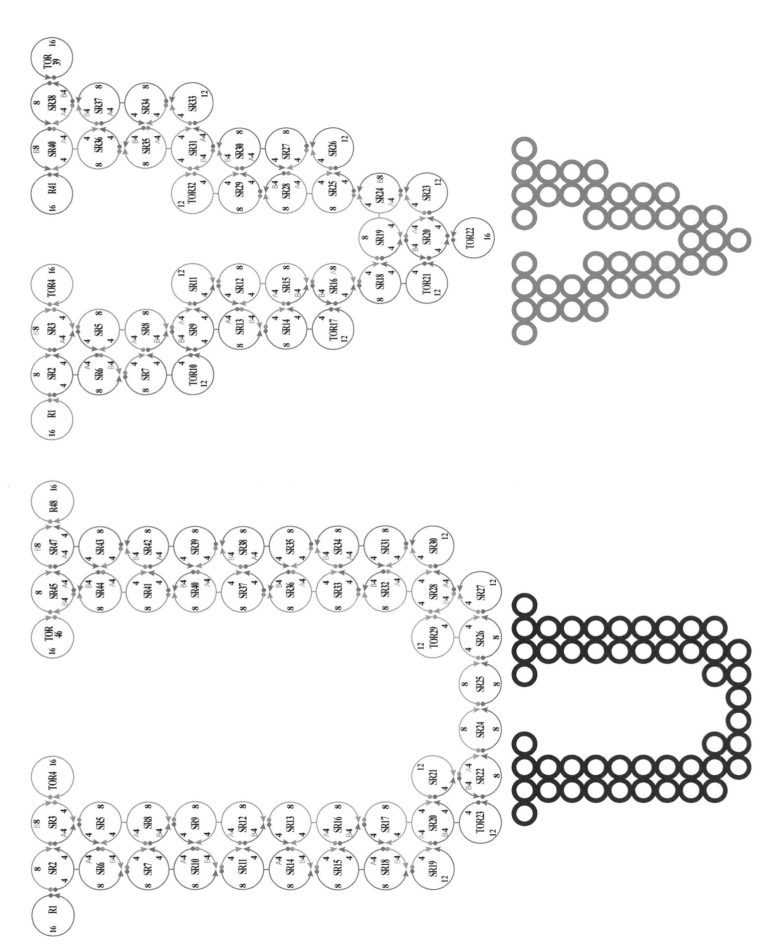

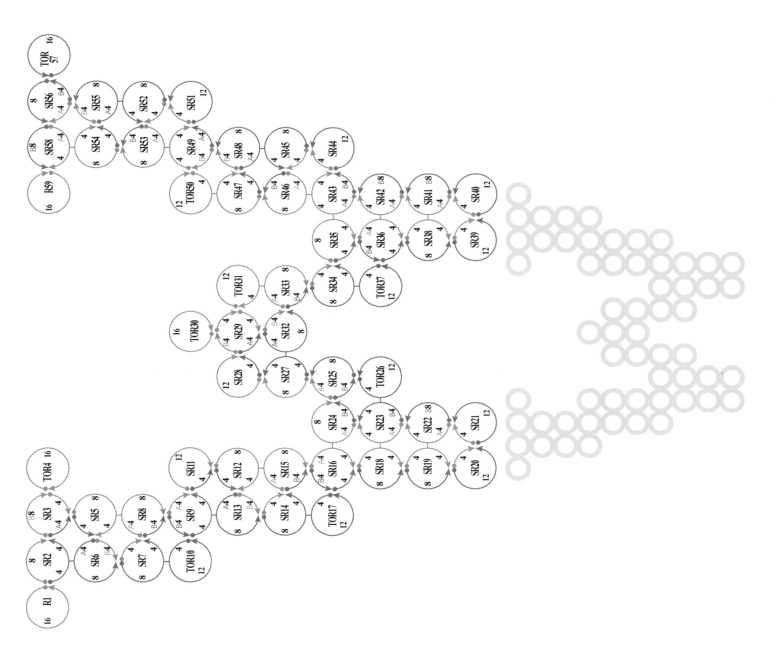

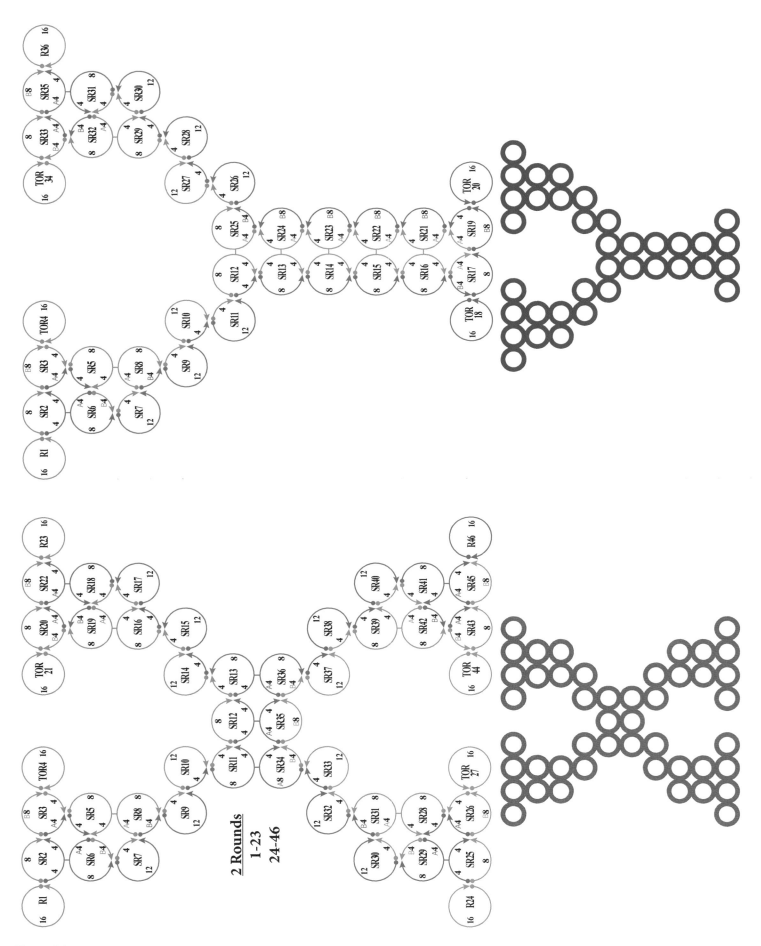

2 Rounds
1-23
24-46

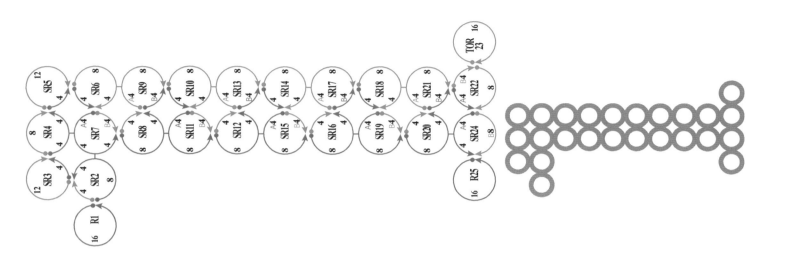

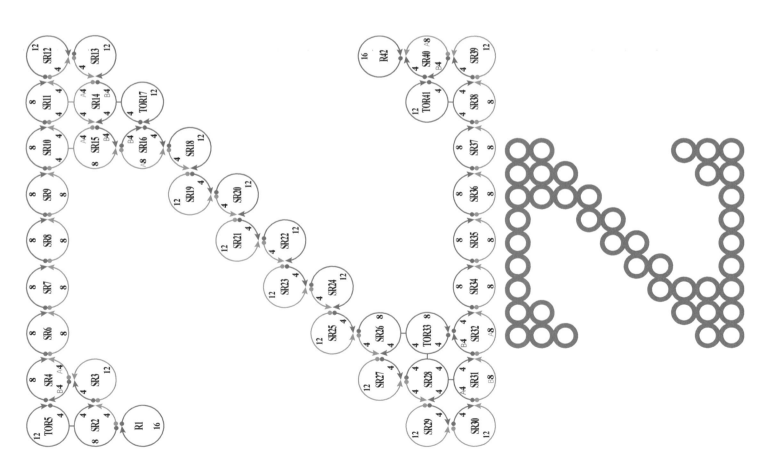

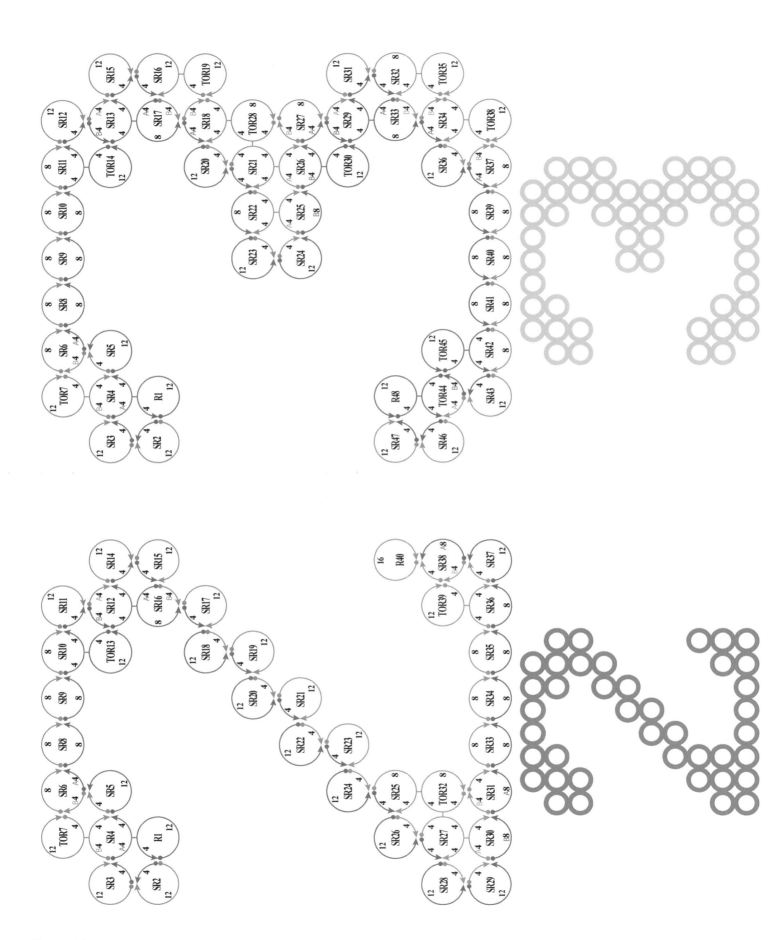

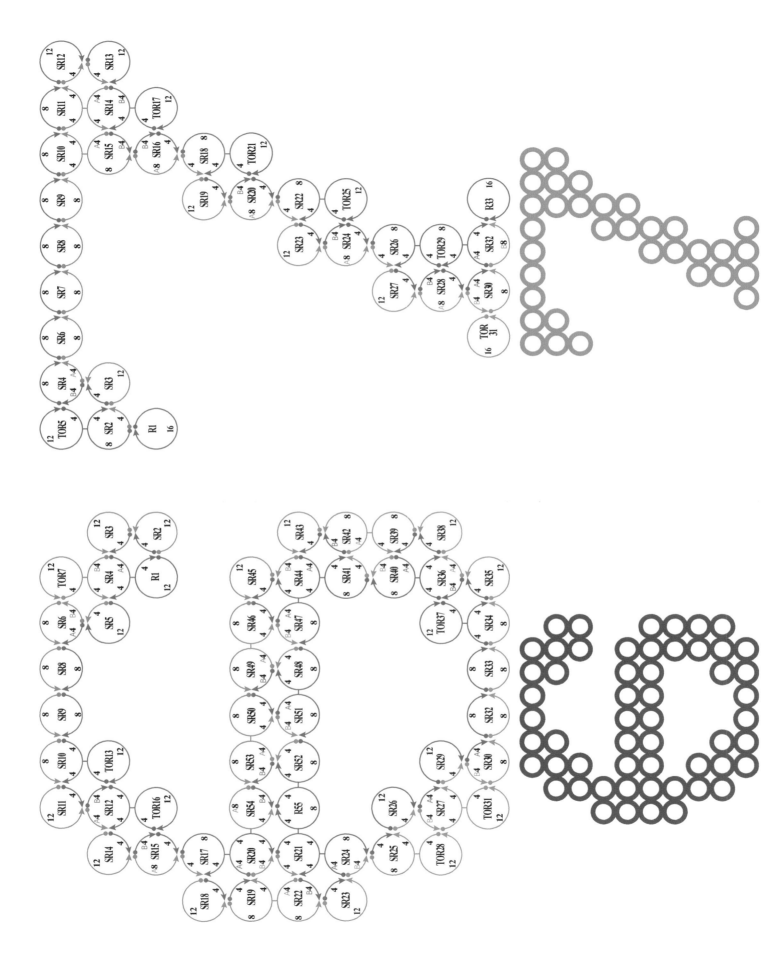

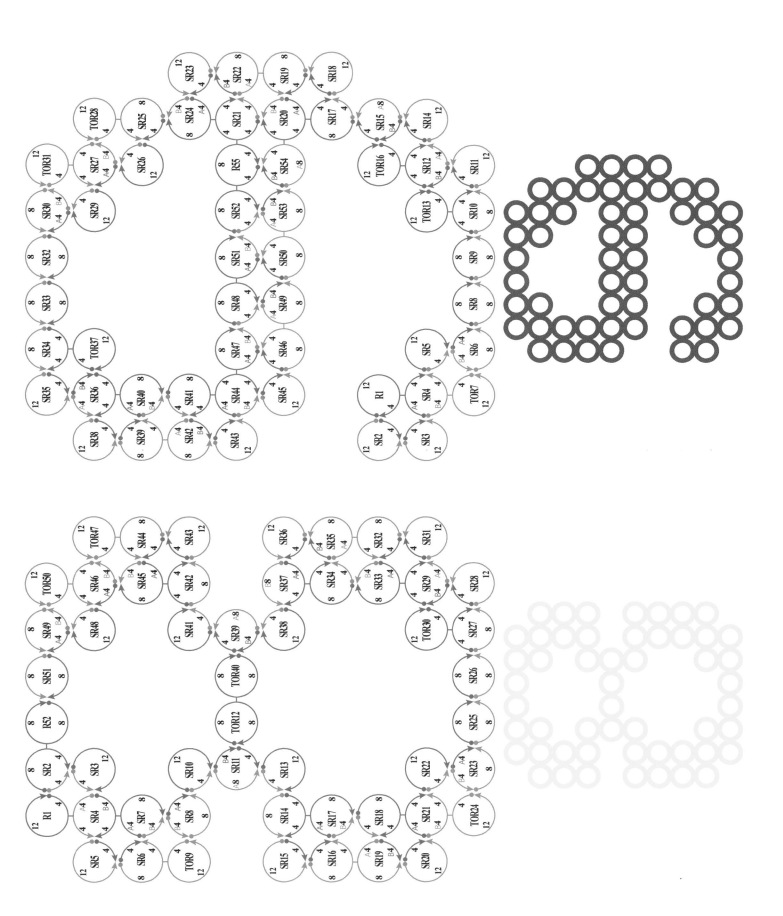

Frames for the Larger Block Alphabet Letters & Numbers--10 Rings High

Frames I through L are created for use with the previous block alphabet letters and numbers.

All letters are 10 rings high.

The width of the letters varies from as little as 4 (I), 5 (1), to as much as 13 (W), M (11).

Most of the letters are 8-10 rings wide with the predominant width being 9.

Frame I

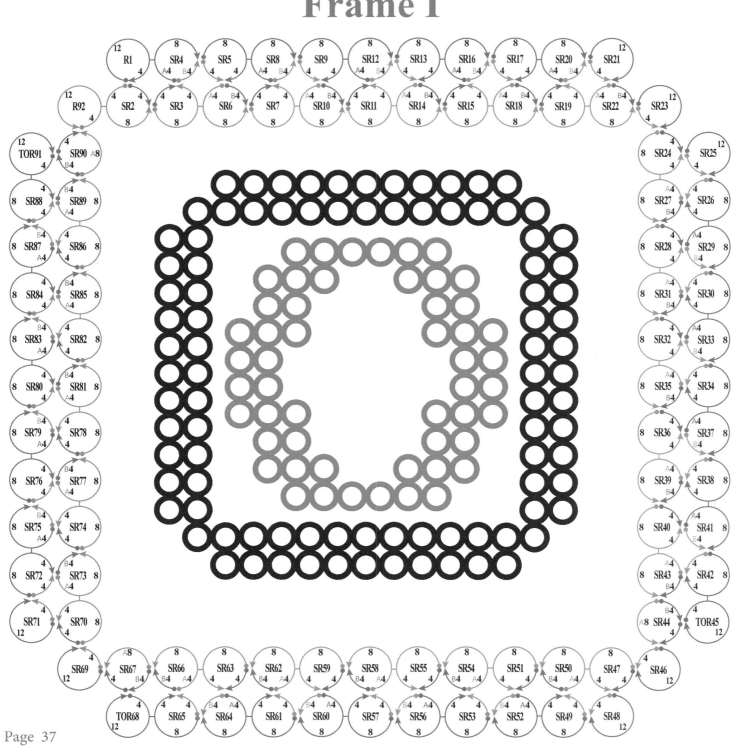

WIDTH
4: I
5: 1
8: J, T, 2, 4, 5, 8
9: B, C, D, E, F, G, H, K, L, P, R, S, V, X, Z, 3, 6, 7, 9
10: A, N, O, Q, U, Y
11: M
13: W

Frames I & J will fit letters up to 10 rings wide.

M & W will NOT fit.

Frame J

Frame K

Frame K will fit letters up to 9 rings wide.

Letters A, M, N, O, Q, U, W, Y will not fit.

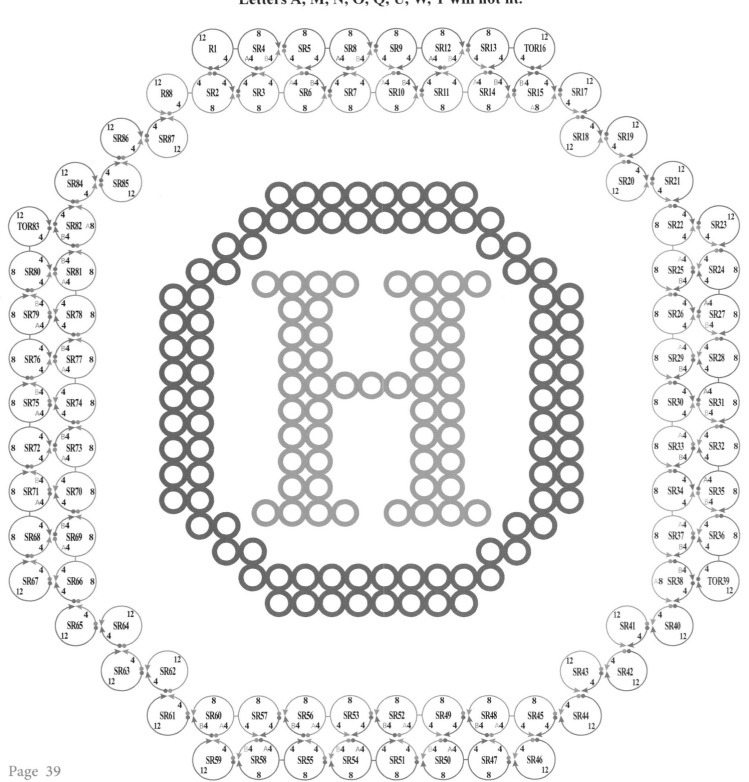

Frame L

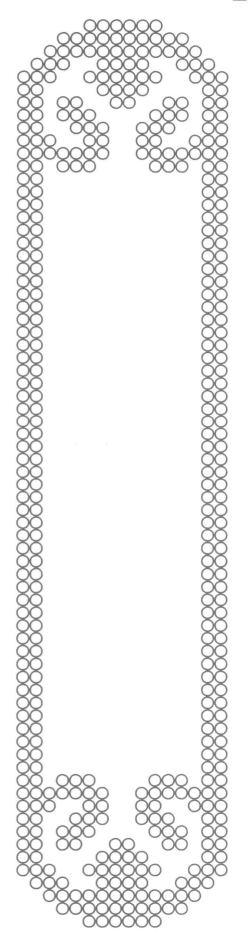

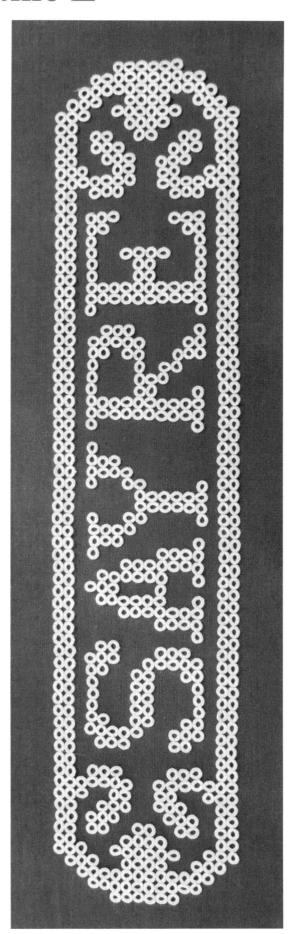

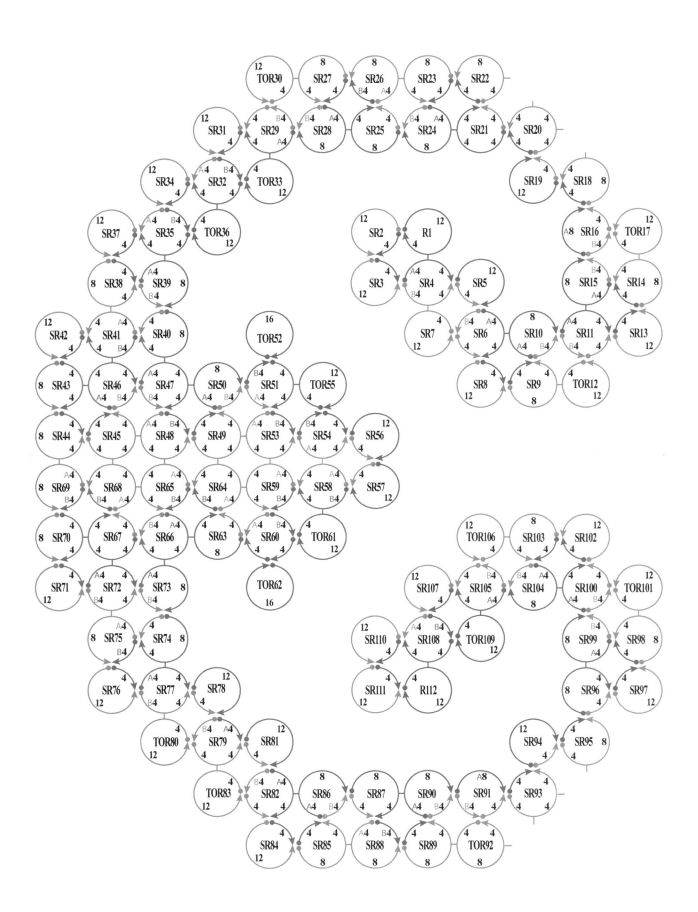

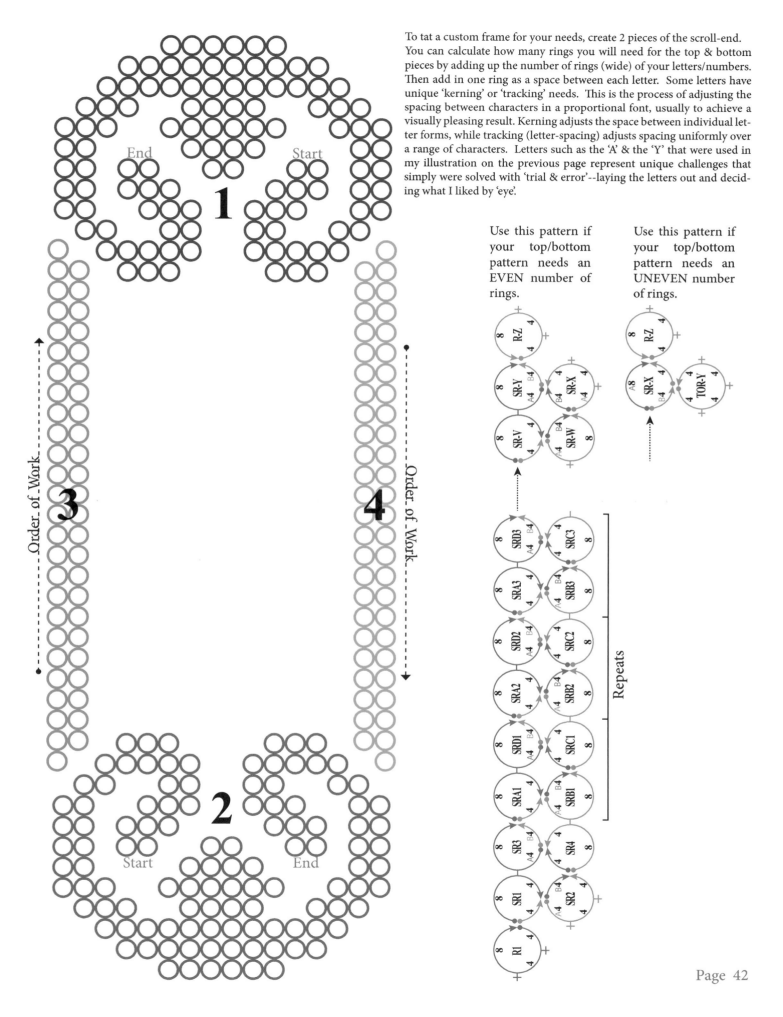

To tat a custom frame for your needs, create 2 pieces of the scroll-end. You can calculate how many rings you will need for the top & bottom pieces by adding up the number of rings (wide) of your letters/numbers. Then add in one ring as a space between each letter. Some letters have unique 'kerning' or 'tracking' needs. This is the process of adjusting the spacing between characters in a proportional font, usually to achieve a visually pleasing result. Kerning adjusts the space between individual letter forms, while tracking (letter-spacing) adjusts spacing uniformly over a range of characters. Letters such as the 'A' & the 'Y' that were used in my illustration on the previous page represent unique challenges that simply were solved with 'trial & error'--laying the letters out and deciding what I liked by 'eye'.

Use this pattern if your top/bottom pattern needs an EVEN number of rings.

Use this pattern if your top/bottom pattern needs an UNEVEN number of rings.

43894314R00027

Made in the USA
Charleston, SC
11 July 2015